Mayas, Incas, and Aztecs

Wendy Conklin, M.A.

Publishing Credits

Content Consultant
Heather Teague

Associate Editor
Christina Hill, M.A.

Assistant Editor
Torrey Maloof

Editorial Assistants
Deborah Buchanan
Kathryn R. Kiley
Judy Tan

Editorial Director
Emily R. Smith, M.A.Ed.

Editor-in-Chief
Sharon Coan, M.S.Ed.

Editorial Manager
Gisela Lee, M.A.

Creative Director
Lee Aucoin

Cover Designer
Lesley Palmer

Designers
Deb Brown
Zac Calbert
Amy Couch
Robin Erickson
Neri Garcia

Publisher
Rachelle Cracchiolo, M.S.Ed.

Teacher Created Materials

5301 Oceanus Drive
Huntington Beach, CA 92649-1030
http://www.tcmpub.com
ISBN 978-0-7439-0456-8
© 2007 Teacher Created Materials, Inc.
Reprinted 2013

Table of Contents

The Medley in the Ancient Americas

In so many ways, the ancient Americans achieved amazing feats. Three of these groups were the Mayas (MY-uhz), Incas (ING-kuhz), and Aztecs (AZ-teks).

These three groups have many things in common. All of them depended on farming to survive. They worshipped many gods. Their art was skillfully detailed. And, the stonework on their buildings was precise.

They also did some things that made them distinct from one another. While the rest of the world borrowed from old languages, the Mayas created their own. Much of what we know about them comes from their

▼ The ancient Aztec city of Tenochtitlan

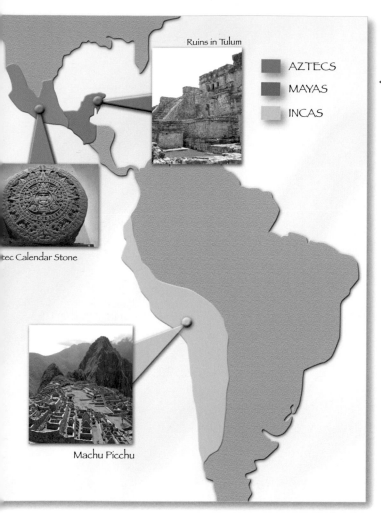

Ruins in Tulum

AZTECS
MAYAS
INCAS

◀ Map showing three of the most important ancient American groups

tec Calendar Stone

Machu Picchu

hieroglyphic (HI-ruh-glif-ik) writing. The Incas constructed more than 10,000 miles (16,000 km) of roads. This made it easy to send messages to all parts of their large empire. Swift messengers sprinted these roads like a relay team. The Aztecs built a city on an island in the middle of a lake. People moved around their city in canoes.

All three groups ended when the Spanish landed in the Americas.

Unearthing the Aztecs

Today, many Aztec ruins lay unseen under cities in Mexico. However, some pyramids can still be seen.

Traveling to the Mayas

If you want to visit the Mayan ruins, you have to go to Honduras, Belize, Guatemala, El Salvador, or southern Mexico.

Trekking the Incas

Each year many tourists go to Peru to see the Incan ruins. Some tourists like to hike up the mountains just as the Incas once did.

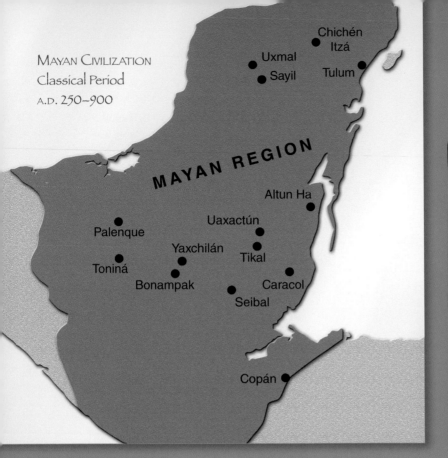

MAYAN CIVILIZATION
Classical Period
A.D. 250–900

MAYAN REGION

Chichén Itzá
Uxmal
Sayil
Tulum
Altun Ha
Uaxactún
Palenque
Yaxchilán
Tikal
Toniná
Bonampak
Caracol
Seibal
Copán

▼ This is a glyph carving.

Meet the Mayas

   Not too long ago, jungles hid the old cities once ruled by Mayan kings. These **city-states** were located on the Yucatán Peninsula (yoo-kuh-TAN puhn-IN-suh-luh). In 1839, two men traveled there from New York. They hoped to find ancient ruins. Led by natives of the land, they found entire cities covered in vines.

   Puzzling **glyphs** (GLIFS) on carved stone monuments greeted them. The Mayas had created their own system of writing that used glyphs. These **steles** (STEE-leez) told the stories of the kings and their people, but no one could read them at first.

◀ Mayan almanac

After some hard work, code breakers were able to make sense of the glyphs. Some glyphs showed how the Mayas kept track of time using two special calendars. One calendar was used for sacred rituals and naming children. It recorded 260 days in its year. The other one had 365 days in a year. It kept track of the movements in the sky. When the sun, planets, and moon moved, the Mayas recorded those movements. They used these records to predict when to go to war, how to farm, and when to host events. The 260-day calendar was the most advanced of any in the world at the time.

Almanacs

The Mayas used their calendars like farmers use **almanacs** (AL-muh-naks). Movements of the sky were noted on their calendars. The Mayas used the calendars to make predictions and keep track of time. Today, farmers' almanacs predict what the weather will be for the year.

Mayan Mathematicians

Mayan priests recorded information about the sky using their own number system. A dot stood for one, a horizontal line represented five, and a shell represented zero.

▲ The rain god was very important to Mayan farmers.

Budding Beliefs

The Mayas were especially good at farming. They enriched the dirt with fertilizers (FUHR-tuhl-iz-uhrz). They used **terraces** (TAIR-ruhs-es) to grow crops on hillsides. To keep the soil from losing its nutrients, they rotated crops like chilies and beans. Some Mayas even grew their own gardens. Their main crop was corn, which grew in several varieties.

One treat they enjoyed was chocolate. It came from beans found in the **cacao** (kuh-KOW) trees in the rain forest. The beans were ground or roasted and mixed into a spicy drink with chilies.

Cacao pod ▶

Because farming was so crucial to them, the Mayas worshipped the gods of nature. The rain god and corn god had temples dedicated to them. The Mayas thought the gods controlled every part of life. To earn the gods' favor, priests made offerings to them in their temples.

▼ This hut is built just like the ancient Mayan huts.

Chocolate

The Spanish took chocolate back to Europe. Back then, it tasted bitter because it did not have any sugar in it.

"Maya" I Have Seconds?

Today we enjoy foods like pineapples, avocadoes, and papaya. So did the Mayas.

Home Sweet Home

Commoners lived in thatched huts supported by poles. These huts had small rooms, including kitchens.

Take Me Out to the Ball Court

The Mayas played the very first team sport. They used a ball made from rubber. The rubber was taken from a tree found in the rain forest. Each team had between two and seven players. The players faced each other. The players tried to keep the ball in play by hitting it with their arms, thighs, and hips. Belts, gloves, and kneepads protected players from the hard falls and the hard ball.

Shaped like the letter *I*, the ball court had a dividing line along the middle. It also had two end zones. Two sloping walls came down to

▼ You can see the sloping walls in the ruins of this ball court.

the middle area. Players bounced the ball off these walls. Many courts even had stone rings that extended from the walls. Some historians wonder if the goal of the game was to hit the ball through the stone rings.

Fans sat on top of the sloped walls as they enjoyed the game with their families. The players dressed up for a pregame ceremony. They wore sandals and headdresses. Music from drums and shelled trumpets blared as the crowds cheered on their favorite teams.

Aztec Ball Games

The Aztecs had ball courts, too. In fact, one city had 11 of them. They played this game, but it is not known for sure if they followed the same rules as the Mayas.

How We Get Rubber

Rubber plantations today cut the bark of rubber trees diagonally. Latex (LAY-teks) seeps out of the tree through these cuts. The latex forms rubber. Rubber is used to make things bouncy.

◀ This marker was used in the ball game.

Mayan Metropolis

In all, the Mayas built more than 100 cities. Each city-state had its own ruler. It was not uncommon for kings to fight one another. At times, they took prisoners and sacrificed them. Other times, these prisoners had to play ball against their own home teams.

The kings commissioned art and buildings to make their cities great. Mayan engineers built these amazing cities without metal tools. One city, Palenque (pah-LENG-kay), even had an **aqueduct** (AK-wuh-duhkt).

Glyphs covered places throughout the city. One stairway in Copán (ko-PAWN) has more than 2,500 glyphs. Some of these glyphs tell Mayan **myths**.

▼ The temples in Tikal are tourist sites today.

▲ The steps going up the Pyramid of the Magician are very steep.

It was very common for cities to have more than one temple. Some temples towered 10 stories into the air. They looked much like pyramids that had steps leading to the top. The temples in Tikal (tee-KAWL) were the steepest in **Mesoamerica**.

It is not known exactly what happened to this great **civilization** (siv-uh-luh-ZAY-shuhn). Close to 1,000 years ago, the Mayas abandoned their cities. The **descendents** (dih-SEN-duhntz) of the Mayas still live in Central America today.

Uxmal

Uxmal (ush-MAWL) had a few interesting buildings: the Pyramid of the Magician and the Nunnery. The Spanish gave the Nunnery its name. It was actually a palace with four sides and a courtyard in the middle. The ruins of both these places can be seen today.

Star Wars

A scene in "Star Wars Episode 4" was filmed at Tikal, Guatemala (gwaw-tuh-MAW-luh). It showed the pyramids peeking out from the jungle. Tikal was the largest city the Mayas built.

Unknown Ending

There are many theories today that tell what happened to the Mayas. Some historians think they overworked the soil and could not farm it anymore. Others say that they were defeated little by little by other kings.

Introducing the Incas

About 500 years ago, the Incas built an empire. It stretched over a long mountain chain known as the Andes (AN-deez) Mountains. Some Incas lived in cities in the valleys and others lived in the mountains.

To stay in touch with such a large population in a big area, they built roads. In fact, they built 10,000 miles (16,000 km) of roads. Messengers ran on these roads carrying news from place to place. In just one day, relay teams could cover 250 miles (400 km). To make it easier to travel through the mountains, they also built bridges. These suspension (suh-SPEN-shuhn) bridges were made from rope and could be stretched 330 feet (100 km).

Most of the Incas lived in homes built from **stucco** (STUH-ko). Those who lived in the mountains did not have enough flat land to

▼ The Incan homes were close together.

Farming terraces ▶

farm. So, they farmed the land by terracing the sides of the mountains. Potatoes and corn were among their main crops. The cold, dry climate allowed them to freeze-dry their food and store it for future use. In this way, there was always enough food for everyone.

Paying Taxes

The Incas paid taxes by working on public works projects. This type of work included building roads and terracing hillsides. Today, people pay taxes by having money taken from paychecks.

Where in the World Are the Incas?

The Incas lived in what is known today as Peru in South America. Many of their descendents still live in the cities and hillsides of the area.

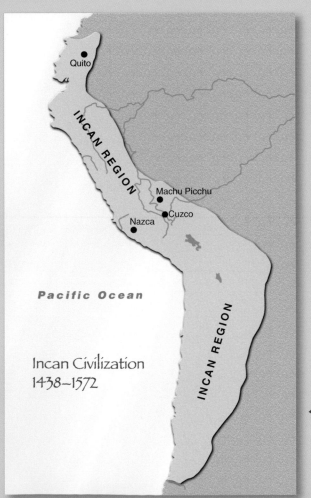

Quito

INCAN REGION

Machu Picchu

Nazca Cuzco

Pacific Ocean

INCAN REGION

Incan Civilization
1438–1572

◀ This map of the Incan region shows a few key cities.

15

Secrets from the Past

Mummies tell the story of the Incas who lived long ago. The Incas wrapped their dead in many layers of cotton. In each layer, they placed items that belonged to that person. Some of these mummies had so many items that they weighed more than 500 pounds (240 kg). The dry air preserved these mummies. Some still have skin, eyes, and fingernails.

Amazingly, the Incas did not have a written language. But, they still managed to keep track of things with a unique system that used strings and knots. These knotted strings made up a *quipu* (KEY-poo). The *quipu* readers used these strings to keep track of how many animals and crops the Incas had. They also told how many people lived in a town and

▼ Machu Picchu is high in the Andes.

who was married. Each village had readers who were the keepers of the knots. They alone knew how to read the messages hidden in the knots on the strings.

One important Incan site is called Machu Picchu (MAW-choo PEE-choo). No one disturbed Machu Picchu over the years. So, the ruins are in very good shape. This town had **ceremonial** (ser-uh-MOH-nee-uhl) stones, drinking fountains, and temples.

▼ Mummies tell people today about ancient Incan life.

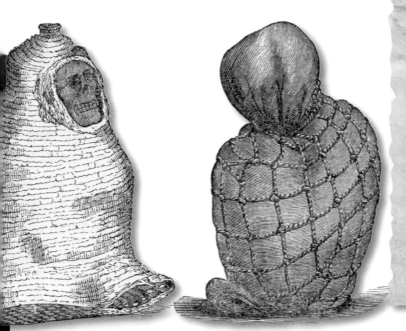

New Findings

Most *quipus* were used for counting items. But recently, researchers are discovering that there are other knots hidden beneath the top knots. In this way, the Incas sent secret messages along the long roads.

Mummies Under Your Feet

The people living in Peru like to learn new things about the Incas from long ago. Just recently, one town found out they were living on a cemetery. In fact, they found more than 2,000 mummies when they tried to install plumbing for the town.

Incas Rule!

The Incas were ruled by a leader called the Sapa Inca. Under him were four governors who each ruled one part of the empire. Each of them had 10 district rulers. The district rulers managed 10,000 people each. These rulers had village leaders who were each in charge of 1,000 people. A village leader relied on 10 workers. Each worker supervised 100 people. Finally, each of these people took care of 10 others. In this way, the Sapa Inca kept a close watch on his people.

The Incas worshipped gods closely tied to nature. Among them were the gods of lightning, thunder, and mountains. The sun god was the one who controlled the success and failure of their crops. The Incas believed their Sapa Inca was a descendent of the sun god, Inti. At times priests offered human **sacrifices** (SAK-ruh-fice-ez) to please the gods.

When the Spanish first set foot in Peru, they brought diseases with them. Even the Sapa Inca died because of disease. A civil war broke out between two of the Sapa

Inca's sons. They both wanted to rule the empire, but the land was too small for such large egos. Atahualpa (aw-tuh-WAWL-puh) won and became the new Sapa Inca.

This war weakened the Incas and allowed the Spanish a great opportunity to seize the land. When the Spanish explorer Francisco Pizarro (puh-ZAWR-oh) arrived, he easily captured Atahualpa.

Francisco Pizarro

▼ Atahualpa was killed by Pizarro.

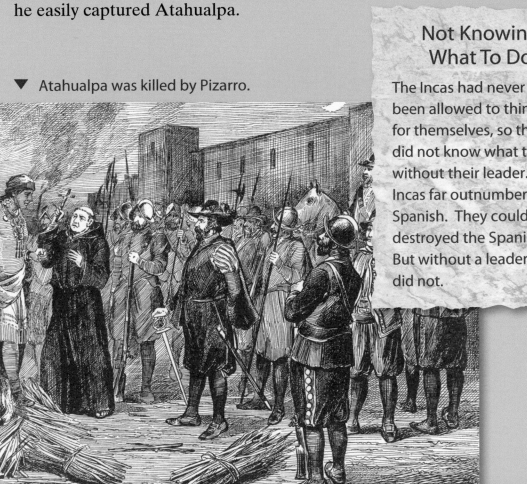

Not Knowing What To Do

The Incas had never been allowed to think for themselves, so they did not know what to do without their leader. The Incas far outnumbered the Spanish. They could have destroyed the Spanish. But without a leader, they did not.

▲ The Aztecs knew to stop when they saw this eagle.

Announcing the Aztecs

Around 1325, a group called the Aztecs decided to move. They did not know where they were going, but their sun god promised to give them land. He said they should live where they saw an eagle sitting on a cactus with a snake. They found this place in central Mexico.

They named their city Tenochtitlan (tay-noch-teet-LAWN). It was located on an island right in the middle of a lake. As it turned out, this location was perfect. They farmed the land by creating floating gardens in the marshland. These gardens were built by grouping twigs together and then adding mud on top. Plant roots often grew into the ground under the water. Among their crops were corn, beans, chilies, and tomatoes.

To get around the city, they used canoes and built canals. They even built highways leading across the lake to the mainland. If war threatened, they simply removed these highways. Their enemies could not reach them unless they had boats. In just a few years, the Aztecs built palaces, temples, ball courts, and even a zoo.

▲ Map of Tenochtitlan

Organizing a City

Aztec cities had sections for each kind of work. Craftsmen, masons, and goldsmiths all had their own parts of the city.

Where Is Tenochtitlan Today?

Tenochtitlan is buried under Mexico City today. Little by little the Aztecs created more dry land with their floating gardens. Since then, the lake has been drained.

Aztec Force

When the Aztecs conquered others around them, they did not force their beliefs on them. They did, however, make others pay a regular tax.

Gods, Myths, and Priests

Like many others, the Aztecs believed in many gods. Because they farmed, the gods of the sun and the rain were important to them. There were temples built for each god on top of a pyramid in Tenochtitlan. Each household had shrines to these gods. People prayed to them daily. Nothing could be done without the approval of the gods.

One god, Quetzalcoatl (ket-sawl-kuh-WAH-tl), looked like a snake with the feathers of a quetzal (ket-SAWL) bird. Their stories tell how he created the world, formed humans, and helped them grow corn. Because there were problems among the gods, he had to leave the Aztecs. But Quetzalcoatl promised he would return one day to help them again.

Special schools called *calmecacs* (kahl-MEH-cahks) were set up to train boys to be priests. Priests had important jobs in the Aztec society. Priests took care of the temples. And, they had to offer sacrifices to the gods. Some of the sacrifices were humans. The priests read the calendar, which pointed to lucky days. Then, they had to decide when to plant crops, build homes, and go to war. The Aztec priests were the decision makers for the cities.

The formal headdresses were made of quetzal feathers.

◀ This Aztec calendar stone is centered around the sun god.

Chocolate Offerings

The Aztecs demanded that their subjects pay a tax to them in cacao beans. One ruler alone brought in about 50 thousand pounds (22,700 kg) of beans each year during his reign. At times these beans were offered as sacrifices to the gods.

Borrowing Mythology

The Aztecs borrowed many myths from earlier people who lived in the area.

Quetzal Bird

The feathers of a quetzal bird were used in Aztec headdresses. These headdresses were worn for special ceremonies. Only one of these headdresses has survived. Some historians believe that it belonged to Moctezuma II (mawk-tuh-ZOO-muh).

▲ This mother teaches her daughter about taking care of the house.

Living the Aztec Life

Aztec cities were broken into sections. Each section had a temple and a leader who served on a council. The council elected one leader to be their Great Speaker.

Women could not hold office. But, they had many of the other freedoms that men enjoyed. Some types of jobs even made Aztec women equal to the priests and nobles.

The Aztecs waged fierce war against others around them. However, they did not have a formal army. Some men were called Eagle Warriors and Jaguar Warriors. These were full-time servicemen. These warriors had the job of guarding

the Great Speaker. They also trained young boys in warfare by showing them how to use weapons. In times of war, the young men reported for service.

The Aztecs loved language. A special group of men received language training. These men composed poetry, riddles, and speeches. They recited some of these poems to the sound of special drumbeats.

Fighting Strategies

The Eagle Warriors and Jaguar Warriors had different fighting tactics. The Eagles always attacked in a group at dawn. The Jaguars waited until their enemies' ranks had broken before taking prisoners.

Battle Gear

Both the Eagle Warriors and Jaguar Warriors were brave in battle. They showed their courage in what they wore on the battlefield. Their headdresses and costumes made them easy to spot as targets. It was a great honor for an enemy to catch one of them in battle.

◄ Aztec warriors ready for battle

Where's the Leader?

In 1502, the council elected a new leader. He was a priest named Moctezuma II. (There was a Moctezuma I, but he is not very well known. So, usually Moctezuma II is just called Moctezuma.) The council members could not find him right away. When they did, he was working in a temple.

As the new leader, Moctezuma strictly enforced the rules of his society. Even if members of his house broke the law, they were punished. Back then, emperors were thought to be weak if they showed compassion. Moctezuma was not weak. To make sure his courts ruled justly, he disguised himself and sat in on court sessions.

To know the future, Moctezuma consulted **necromancers** (NEK-ruh-man-suhrs). Unfortunately, they brought him bad news most of the time. They believed eclipses and meteors were bad **omens**. Moctezuma was afraid that the end of his empire was near. Every night he searched for dreams and signs that would prove these omens wrong.

The year that the Spanish arrived in Tenochtitlan matched with the date of Quetzalcoatl's predicted return. Moctezuma wondered if the Spanish leader, Hernán Cortés, was Quetzalcoatl. Moctezuma let the Spanish enter his capital. He hoped he could learn more about the Spanish. What he learned was that he had made a huge mistake.

Hernán Cortés

Moctezuma's Palace

Today, the president of Mexico has a palace like Moctezuma did. In fact, the palace sits on the same spot where Moctezuma's palace once stood.

Other Visions

Moctezuma's aunt had visions as well. She dreamed that shining white men walked across the water killing many of her people.

Cortés and His Translator

All along, Cortés knew about Moctezuma's struggles. Cortés had a translator named Dona Marina who knew the Aztec language. She told Cortés of the legends of Quetzalcoatl. Some historians today think that Marina was a traitor to the Aztecs.

▼ Doña Marina translates for Cortés.

The Spanish End the Three

No one knows for sure why the Mayan civilization ended. Some think they ran out of food and had to move elsewhere or starve. Others think that warring tribes weakened the city-states. Many of the cities had already died out when the Spanish arrived. The Spanish fought the remaining Mayas and overtook their cities.

The Incas survived until the Spanish explorer Francisco Pizarro arrived in 1532. The nation was fighting a civil war between two brothers. It was a prime time for a small group of explorers to take over. Within 40 years, the Spanish ended the Incan ruling **dynasty** (DIH-nuh-stee). Today, there are still some Incas who live in the region. They speak the language and practice many of the old customs.

▼ Pizarro's men meet with the Incas.

▲ Moctezuma is brought before the Aztecs.

Soon after he arrived in the Aztec empire, Hernán Cortés took Moctezuma prisoner. He used Moctezuma to get gold. After a few months, the Aztecs grew restless and began rioting. The Spanish brought Moctezuma to calm his people, but the Aztecs stoned him to death. In no time, the Spanish took control of the rioting people, and the mighty Aztec empire was no more.

These cultures still have mysteries to solve and stories to tell. People are learning more about them all the time.

The Magnificent Mayas

Today, there are at least four million Mayas still living. Many descendents of the Mayas still live on the Yucatán Peninsula. They protect the ancient sites from long ago and use them to learn more about the Mayan **legacy** (LEG-uh-see).

The Incredible Incas

In many ways, the Incas today have changed very little from their ancestors. Many continue to live in the mountains of Peru. Most of them still farm the same crops and wear the same styles of clothing.

Aztecs Still Alive!

Today, about one million Aztecs still live in Mexico.

Glossary

almanacs—books that help make predictions about things like weather and crops

aqueduct—pipe or channel used to carry water

cacao—beans that are used to make cocoa and chocolate

ceremonial—used in ceremonies or for religious practices

city-states—ancient cities that ruled themselves independently

civilization—a society that has writing and keeps track of records

descendents—relatives of someone from the past

dynasty—a group of rulers from one family

glyphs—picture writing, hieroglyphics

hieroglyphic—writing formed with pictures rather than letters

legacy—something handed down from ancestors or relatives

Mesoamerica—the region that includes Central and South America

myths—stories about the lives of the gods

necromancers—people who consult the dead for help or advice

omens—events that are believed to tell about future events

quipu—knotted strings that kept records in the Incan society

sacrifices—gifts offered to the gods; sometimes human beings were killed

steles—stone monuments with writing on them

stucco—plaster or cement

terraces—areas of flat land on sloping hillsides used for farming

Index

Image Credits